How to Stop Being Jealous

Discover How to Overcome Jealousy Issues and Feel Secure in Your Relationship

by Reena Summers

Table of Contents

Introduction 1

Chapter 1: Understanding Your Situation 7

Chapter 2: How to Rebuild Your Relationship 15

Chapter 3: Letting Go of Jealousy 21

Chapter 4: Sustaining a Healthy Relationship 27

Chapter 5: How to Ensure Success 37

Conclusion 43

Introduction

Let's face it: Occasionally there may be a valid reason for you to feel jealous and resentful because of something that your partner did (or failed to do). Unfortunately, this jealousy in turn affects and strains your relationship. But even worse are situations when the jealousy actually stems from your own feelings of inadequacy or insecurity.

Too often, an otherwise healthy relationship is completely wrecked by too many suspicions and failing trust or faith in the other partner. All because of baseless and unfounded fits of jealousy.

Thus, the focus of this book is to discuss (and eliminate) the latter scenario where we operate on the premise that there is nothing to be jealous about and these pangs of jealousy are only unfounded suspicions that need to be shed and swept away once and for all.

Based on the assumption that the relationship is otherwise secure, stable, and healthy, the jealous partner (most likely *you*, since you're reading this) must learn to be able to contain any raging feelings of jealousy in order to make the relationship survive, thrive, and prosper for a full, secure, and happy life together.

In this book, you will find the help you're looking for, including assistance in developing the skills needed to help you understand the *reality* of your situation through a new perspective; tactics to help you rebuild your relationship and put it on the right path; guidelines for letting go of jealousy once and for all; and tips for sustaining a healthy relationship to ensure future success.

So if you're finally ready to kick the green monster out of your life for good, then let's get started!

© Copyright 2015 by Miafn LLC - All rights reserved.

This document is geared towards providing reliable information in regards to the topic and issue covered. The publication is sold with the idea that the publisher is not required to render accounting, officially permitted, or otherwise, qualified services. If advice is necessary, legal or professional, a practiced individual in the profession should be ordered.

- From a Declaration of Principles which was accepted and approved equally by a Committee of the American Bar Association and a Committee of Publishers and Associations.

In no way is it legal to reproduce, duplicate, or transmit any part of this document in either electronic means or in printed format. Recording of this publication is strictly prohibited and any storage of this document is not allowed unless with written permission from the publisher. All rights reserved.

The information provided herein is stated to be truthful and consistent, in that any liability, in terms of inattention or otherwise, by any usage or abuse of any policies, processes, or directions contained within is solely and completely the responsibility of the recipient reader. Under no circumstances will any legal responsibility or blame be held against the publisher for any reparation, damages, or monetary loss due to the information herein, either directly or indirectly.

Respective authors own all copyrights not held by the publisher.

The information herein is offered for informational purposes solely, and is universal as so. The presentation of the information is without contract or any type of guarantee assurance.

The trademarks that are used are without any consent, and the publication of the trademark is without permission or backing by the trademark owner. All trademarks and brands within this book are for clarifying purposes only and are the owned by the owners themselves, not affiliated with this document.

Chapter 1: Understanding Your Situation

Stop and gain some perspective

Take a deep breath and count from one to ten. This should allow you enough time to calm down. Taking a step back and gaining some perspective is a key skill in dealing with stress. Gaining perspective is the ability to see things from ten paces back.

In your harried everyday life, you are sometimes caught in a whirlwind of activity and concerns that you often neglect to take a step back and pay attention to your emotions and psychological health. Continuously neglecting your emotional and mental health can lead to anger, depression and aggravate your destructive and negative emotions like jealousy.

Sometimes you allow your jealousy to flare up in anger, and you cannot get a grip on yourself. The little green monster rears its ugly head again and all you see is red, and your blood is boiling with all that wrath and fury. Then there is absolutely nothing you can do when you are at that point of no return and in those moments of blind rage, you let out a barrage of words that will probably end your relationship.

All that fury is possibly justified if at that point in time your partner is caught red-handed. However, if you just let yourself go into a blind rage, you may hurt someone physically or say something really uncalled for and damage your relationship.

If you have already experienced similar situations, it is definitely necessary for you to take some time to help ease you into a calmer state of mind. But work on it—maybe start yoga or swimming—and it will be worth the trouble because you will come out more positive and stronger.

Since your goal here is to get rid of your jealous tendencies, it is imperative that you take a good and careful look at the state of your emotional health. When you are done, you will feel lighter inside and be more positive in your outlook on life.

Get a grip on yourself

Look at yourself in the mirror and come face to face with your jealous emotions. Take a few minutes to calm yourself and assess the current situation. Stopping for a moment can help you clear your head and think more rationally so that you will not do or say anything you will later regret.

This is just the beginning of your journey to emotional stability and a jealousy-free existence. If you succeed in this part, then you are already halfway out of the woods. To be able to rid yourself of any negative thoughts that can lead to jealous fits, you must first exert enough time and effort to find a handle on yourself and your emotions.

Do not allow your emotions to take control of you and your life. You do not need to be told how unattractive it is when you let anger and your jealousy consume you. But you should also not let your emotions remain hidden only to let your anger eat you up inside. Emotions are not meant to be locked up, especially not anger stemming from serious pangs of jealousy.

Just like when you clean your house and let the sunlight in, when you start cleaning out your emotions and your emotional baggage, you open yourself up to welcoming new and positive thoughts. Know that in doing so, something wonderful is about to happen to you and your life.

The greatest struggles in human history are not really those fought in the battlefields in the midst of the greatest wars. Rather, the greatest human struggles are those within each and every one of us. In your case, your current and greatest struggle is to deal with jealousy and all its negativity, and to defeat it.

Recognize and reset your jealousy triggers

First, you have to understand your anger and what triggers your strong negative emotions. Emotions are natural and common individual human reactions to day-to-day things. But emotions, no matter how fleeting, can damage even a perfectly good relationship.

We all have different means of reacting to situations and coping with anger and its backlash. Some react by just going into a blind rage while others keep the rage and the hurt inside themselves. Either way, whether you go into a jealous rampage or lock up in secret your jealous feelings, sooner or later you will hurt your partner, yourself and your relationship in the long run.

So, just like every other person, you need to first understand what you are feeling and what triggers your emotions particularly your anger and jealous rage in order to better manage and even prevent these emotions in the future. Your objective now is to help yourself put the lost, missing, broken and confusing pieces of your life together in order for you to take control of your emotions and of your life. Steel yourself when the jealousy alarm is set off.

The process will definitely not be easy. You will have to go through every inch of your emotions. You will have to clean up the hot mess of rage and negativity and plug up the leaks of your failing confidence and self-esteem. You will need to clear out the debris of your doubts and suspicions. You will have to oil the squeaks of your unhealthy relationship and reveal and repair any damage in your emotional state.

Express your emotions

Keeping your strong negative emotions locked up could eventually lead to adverse effects on your mental and even your physical health. Some adverse effects of your negative emotions include colds and flu, serious coronary heart disease, stroke, depression, high blood pressure, severe anxiety, stress, gastrointestinal problems and paranoia. Aside from these, your pent-up emotions could drive you to harm yourself, to alcohol or substance abuse, or even make you contemplate suicide.

Thus, you need to find healthy ways of expressing or releasing your anger such as breathing deeply, meditating, exercising and confiding in someone you trust. In the succeeding chapters, we will further explore those ways in which you take control of your emotions.

Communicate with your partner or a close confidant about your feelings

Once you have sufficiently given yourself time to pause and breathe, talk to your spouse or partner. You need to express yourself constructively and positively. Talk to your spouse or partner about what's eating you. Chances are, he or she may not even be aware if you hide what you are feeling inside. Expressing yourself does not mean going on a rampage or letting the green-eyed monster transform you into a raving lunatic.

Talk to the other person in a calm manner and avoid raising your voice or sounding confrontational. Talking in a calm tone of voice somehow soothes you and assures the other person that you intend to settle the issue peacefully. Explain your feelings and what led you to your anger and ask for an explanation for the behavior that triggered your anger. Talking can thresh out the issue at hand faster than sweeping it under the rug first and allowing your emotions to escalate and then explode later on.

Bear in mind that if you succeed in clearing out your emotional cobwebs and debris, you will be able to lay down a foundation of confidence, love and support for yourself and eventually build a more solid base for your relationship with your partner.

Chapter 2: How to Rebuild Your Relationship

Check your relationship's health status

Recognize that your relationship with your partner is not and will never be a placid lake. In reality, your relationship changes constantly in the same way that you and your partner evolve as individuals over time.

Thus, conflict in a relationship is bound to crop up at some point. Conflict in a relationship comes and goes. Some instances are due to the sad reality that couples fail to meet each other's needs. Couples become frustrated because of repeated disappointments. Sometimes, couples make each other unhappy, even by deliberately hurting each other.

Know and understand each other's needs

Now that you have gone through the process of dissecting your emotions and recognizing the jealousy triggers, you and your partner can start to rebuild your relationship. Continue communicating with each other about what triggers the episodes of jealous rages and avoid those pitfalls. Then, discuss with your partner how you can move forward from there.

To communicate well with your partner, you also need to discuss each other's most important emotional needs. Knowing and understanding your partner's needs will allow you to address those needs. Ignorance of your partner's needs is the source of the failure to care and address those particular needs.

This is because men and women have great difficulty understanding and appreciating the value of each other's needs. Acknowledge your differences. Men tend to try to meet needs that they would value and women tend to do the same. The problem is that the needs of men and women are often very different and we waste effort trying to meet the wrong ends.

You and your partner should level with each other and identify your important emotional needs. Once you have identified your most important emotional needs, communicate them clearly to each other and learn to meet these needs fully.

Always strive to meet each other's needs

Often, it is when your needs are unmet that you become thoughtless and inconsiderate of your partner. Then you slide into patterns that hurt and take each other for granted. Later on, these patterns turn into bad habits of hurting the other sometimes even out of spite. However, the failure to meet needs is often unintentional, but the reaction to unmet needs develops into intentional harm. Then the relationship slides into ugly and destructive scenes and jealous rage. Eventually this cycle of hate and hurt leads to unbearable pain and ultimately divorce or breakup.

Successful relationships require skill in understanding and caring for your partner. Good intentions and words are not enough. So whether you just started your life together, have had an average relationship for a number of years, have a bad marriage or relationship or even had an affair, you can rebuild your relationship, if you become aware of each other's needs and learn to meet them.

Always strive to keep your love alive

The longest and strongest relationships are often not the ones kept with the grandest gestures. Instead, it is the littlest and most common and ordinary things that continue to keep the flames of love burning and the relationship going. Remember that to love someone is always to wish that person the best. So, always wish the best for each other.

Do not forget to strive to always be in a loving state, even if not always feeling that original state of being in love. This is easier said than done when you have been together for a considerable amount of time. It is harder still if you have been driven apart by many instances of doubt and recrimination and jealous rages.

Remember to always show affection. Hold each other's hand—this doesn't have to be in public. Kiss each other inside the elevator. Hold your partner's hand at the movies. Tell your wife she looks beautiful. Tell your boyfriend he looks dashing in his new coat. Give each other compliments from time to time.

Do not speak ill of your partner to family or friends. Even when you need to unload your feelings of doubt and suspicion, choose only your closest friends to confide in. Resist the urge to publicly shame your partner even if he or she is indeed guilty of infidelity.

Listen to each other. Admit your faults and mistakes. When you are the one wrong, say that you are sorry. When you are right, resist the urge to gloat, and just be quiet instead. Do not raise your voices at each other, especially not in front of children. Yell only when the house is burning or your dog has gone missing or your neighbor is dying. Most importantly, on the days when you are consumed by doubt and loathing, try to remember that you love each other.

Chapter 3: Letting Go of Jealousy

Get rid of every jealous bone in your body.

Jealousy can undoubtedly be hurtful. It is a very strong emotion and its effects far-reaching and disturbing in a relationship. Jealousy is intense and can sour your relationship and even your outlook on life for some time.

The good news is that jealousy can also be helpful even if it is hurtful. Even if you are suffering from intense pangs of jealousy at any given point in time, you can will yourself to minimize your feelings and direct yourself to convert it to other feelings that are painless and constructive.

Come to realize that you have no need to be jealous or fearful of a rival for your partner's love and attention. Learning to harness your feelings of jealousy will eventually strengthen your character and you will be better able to cope with it. You may not be able to rid yourself entirely of every jealous bone in your body, but you can definitely change your attitude towards jealousy and learn to cope with it.

Learn to let go of your old patterns of jealousy and insecurity

Instead, create your own positive patterns. Will yourself to channel only positivity and beauty, and let go of all those negative thoughts. You are what you think you are and what you think you can accomplish.

Instead of thinking that something is bound to go wrong and your partner will wind up cheating on you, let go of all those bad vibes. Focus instead on improving yourself, your health, your career, your finances—everything.

Let go of the doubt and the paranoia and think instead that people are meant to be trusted and that they deserve your trust. Remember that your life changes when you yourself change for the better.

Take a step back and take a deep breath

Breathe slowly and regularly. This is one of the fastest ways to trigger the body's relaxation response. Studies also suggest that almost any spiritual practice such as attending service, saying prayers, yoga and meditation induces relaxation by slowing the heart rate via controlled breathing.

Rate stressful situations on a one-to-ten scale, with ten being a catastrophic event like a death, and not your partner flirting with the stranger. This helps put minor annoyances into perspective. And gaining that perspective allows you to cope with more stress while feeling less stressed out.

Organize your life

You have recognized that the environment you live in has piled up so much pressure and stress on you and your outlook on life. The physical, emotional and social demands of your life seem to multiply unendingly. Every day, the hectic, demanding and tiring events coupled with the psychological pressures all combine to heap unexpected stress on you. If you examine your life and the pressures that you have to contend with, it is no joke that sometimes you turn into Godzilla or the Incredible Hulk when your buttons are pushed and your rage and jealousy triggered.

Organization can be the key to your survival. If things seem to be getting on top of you, sit down and take stock of the situation before you are swept away in a storm of rage and trauma once more.

When you are planning your life, try dividing up things you have to think about into three or four areas such as work, family, your partner and you. The fourth category is one of the most important but is usually undervalued.

So organize your life but always remember to set aside adequate quality time for yourself. Just as you look after your family, your work, your partner, you need to also look after your own needs. Make sure that you put aside a little time every day to relax and indulge yourself. If you take care of yourself, you will not feel cheated or robbed. You will be able to find calm within yourself and not feel grumpy, irritable or jaded.

Create your own space

All you need is a very small area to create a space that is yours and yours alone. Everyone needs a spot where they can tune out their daily obligations to listen to their heart's longings and desires. Call it your antidote to the super speed that you normally operate at for the rest of the day.

Make it a room all your own whether it is for tinkering with your tools or sewing a dress or a quilt. It can be a small area tucked into an attic or carved out of your bedroom. It can be your meditation room and writing room. It is your very own spot, where you can find solace, inspiration, clarity and focus and find yourself.

Chapter 4: Sustaining a Healthy Relationship

Love, love, love

It is no secret that love is the foundation of healthy and happy relationships. Without it, a relationship cannot thrive. Yet, many mistake love for a feeling when it is actually an act. Often though, too much love is what leads to intense pangs of jealousy. Loving is a verb, an action word that requires a choice. It does not pop out all of a sudden in our heads and in our hearts. Love starts with a choice. Love starts with a commitment to do exactly that, to love.

Renew your commitment

To commit to love someone means you have to keep at it even when times are tough and rough sailing. Loving your partner means you have to continue trying to keep the fire alive even when your present feelings do not necessarily agree and correspond with the challenge to love. Learning to love unconditionally is a process and not something you can do in neat boxes and in the blink of an eye. So if you want your relationship to grow and continue to be healthy, you must start with yourself.

Bury the past and move on

Weed out the enemies of a good and lasting relationship. Stop verbally punishing your spouse or partner for misdeeds or acts of infidelity. Stop using words that are designed to hurt each other such as name-calling. Do not lose control even when you are provoked and there is another situation where jealousy is about to rear its ugly head.

Resentment from past verbal battles cause a couple to hate each other. If you feel angry and resentful, express your feelings and describe your expectations to your partner. But remember not to use verbal punishment ever again. It only makes your partner angry and resentful and much less willing to meet your needs in the future.

Make your own brand of love

The nice thing about learning to love is that even if you were not raised in a healthy loving environment, you still have the option and the choice to start nurturing such pure love in your own relationship. With your own relationship, now that you are reclaiming your love, you can make your own fresh start.

Learn to accept and love yourself first

To do this, you must first start to learn to forgive and love yourself before you can be equipped to send love signals to your spouse or partner. Do this even if you need to seek professional help. Sometimes, confiding in a devoted friend or your partner will provide inner healing.

You should try to seek whatever means work for you in trying to improve your emotional well-being, particularly in overcoming your intense feelings of jealousy. It is the first and most important step towards keeping your love and your relationship alive and healthy.

Communication is key

Talk to your partner regularly. Air your sentiments. Communication is the foundation for a successful relationship. Caring partners converse in a caring way. Listen to what your partner says and not just what you want to hear. It is very easy to miscommunicate and to get our wires crossed. Some miscommunications are easy to clear up, some are not. Other miscommunications can take a little longer to clear up but it is imperative to clear them up because if they are left unresolved, they could eventually destroy your relationship.

Commit to communicating constantly, clearly and lovingly with your partner. Remember the old saying about sticks and stones breaking one's bones? Well, words can indeed make or break someone. It is true, sticks and stones may hurt physically. But they do not have the power to deeply damage spirits, much less lovingly heal hearts. Words do.

In any relationship, it is truly important to be careful about what is being said. Harsh words can cause the death of a heart, which goes to show how small but powerful the tongue is. At some point, you and your partner are guilty of misusing your tongue and lashing out at each other, especially if you are stuck in one of your jealous fits. Thus, be careful of the words you utter especially when you are mad and jealous. In these circumstances it is better to take time out and learn to return when you are able to use your words to infuse joy and laughter instead of discouraging and destroying your partner's feelings and confidence. You will know when you are doing this right, because you will be making yourself feel better as well.

Give each other undivided attention

The conversation a woman needs from her partner requires undivided attention. It is recommended that each week, each couple should set aside around 15 hours for the purpose of giving each other their undivided attention. Converse with each other. Do not watch a football game or a basketball game or a movie during that time. Those of you, who simply can't imagine suddenly beginning to speak for such prolonged periods, can start by doing a peaceful activity together like playing chess or going for a walk. Even start a hobby that could create avenues for mutual interests and naturally lead up to developing the habit of talking again.

Balance the conversation with your partner

Those who monopolize the conversation create an unwanted habit in their partner—silence. Always try to give each other enough time to have the floor, so to speak. Therefore, if you want to have a good conversation with your partner, be sensitive to each other's right to "have the floor."

It may sometimes take a few seconds for the other to begin a sentence, but allow whatever time is necessary. And remember to wait until your partner completes a thought before commenting on it. Learn to balance your conversation. Avoid interrupting each other and try to give each other the same amount of time to talk.

Use your time for conversation to inform, investigate and understand your partner. One of the most valuable uses of conversation in a relationship is to create emotional closeness. Choose your topics of conversation well. The topics of your conversation also have a great bearing on the intimacy of your relationship. Develop interest in each other's favorite topics of conversation.

Never use conversation as a form of punishment such as ridiculing your partner, name calling, swearing and sarcasm. Conversations with your partner should be constructive, not destructive.

Declutter your mind and your relationship

You need to be just as conscientious about tossing out old things that clutter up your relationship, such as old hurts, unfinished arguments and unforgivingness. They only take up room in our minds and drain us of the energy needed for the more important things and events in life.

Whatever clutter is clogging up your mind, your hearts and your relationship, you should be doing your best to get rid of it. Instead, give your relationship the care it needs. Remove the clutter like jealous emotions immediately before they stifle you and your partner and destroy your relationship.

Remember how it was when you just started dating. You both still need to exhibit the same interest in each other and in what you have to say especially about your feelings.

Much like a plant that you lovingly plant and care for, your relationship can only thrive with proper care. Your relationship needs tender loving care, the right amount of sunlight and water, nourished with the right amount of love and understanding. If your needs and those of your partner are met, your relationship will thrive and bloom to its fullest.

Chapter 5: How to Ensure Success

Wave the red flag and conquer the jealousy bull

Jealousy is one of the facts of life and cannot be completely prevented in any relationship. Deal with your jealousy by waving the red flag when you see it and retuning your attitude. Your attitude is one of the first things people notice about you. While you may not be able to change your height or body type, you can definitely change your attitude.

Changing your attitude about your partner and coping with jealousy is one important step to changing your attitude and approach in life. If your attitude is bad, it can be better. With proper awareness and daily training, you can harness your feelings and divert your feelings of jealousy and insecurity. If your attitude is already good, you can even make it better, much greater than it already is.

So, every now and then subject yourself to an emotional and attitude tune-up in order to keep your jealous tendencies in check. If you have not been getting your life and your relationship where you want it, then a maintenance check-up is definitely in order. The good news is that there are more tools that you can put to good use. One example is the use of affirmation and self-motivation. Use these tools and refine and retune your attitude regularly in order to take control of your life and drive away your jealousy demons.

Motivate yourself constantly

Use affirmations. These are tools for self-motivation. Use these affirmations to tell yourself the things you wish to accomplish like banishing worry and anxiety. Tell yourself that there is nothing to doubt and be suspicious of. Affirmations repeated over and over can reprogram your mind into positive thinking. Continue motivating yourself and soon you will discover the real power of affirmations. Think along the lines of the mantra of Muhammad Ali: "I am the greatest!" Or the slogan of Nike telling you to "Just Do It!" Keep repeating your affirmations and feel your confidence grow. Soon you will realize that you have outgrown your jealous tendencies and you trust that all is well with your relationship.

Always strive to improve yourself

You have been focusing on your internal health such as your emotional handle and your attitude so far. So seek other ways to constantly improve yourself. Start with the most obvious ones like your hair or your weight. Get a makeover. Buy a new wardrobe.

If you ask why, the simple answer is because there is only one you. So why not be the absolute best version of yourself that you can be. This is your life and your moment. It is well worth your time and your energy to be as self-expressed and as happy and as beautiful as you can possibly be.

Beauty includes the physical appearance but it does not stop there. Beauty is the result of a quality of being, not the result of the arrangement of physical characteristics. True beauty demands more than a great body or a cute face. True beauty demands that you treat yourself and others well.

Beauty asks that you be kind, generous, forgiving and gracious. Beauty insists that you develop your mind as well as your figure. Cultivate your self-worth and make it grow. Find the courage to make a change if you need it. No matter how slight or drastic the change, the possibilities are exciting and endless. There is nothing arrogant or vain about trying to be as beautiful as you can possibly be.

Trying to be the best you can be is in fact a noble cause because the image you project to the world often reflects what people cannot see, what is inside of you. Being beautiful is about cultivating your greatest intellectual and spiritual attributes in order for you to evolve into your very best self. There has always been a natural synergy between improving physically and improving mentally, emotionally and spiritually.

So get moving and be on the road to start your journey to becoming the best person you can become. Be the best you can be, not just physically, but in every way.

Continue finding yourself and discovering your purpose

Relying on outside motivation is kind of like listening to a marching band. While the marching band is playing its music, the music will get you to your feet and gel you to move to the beat. But once the music stops, you feel lost and alone. This is when you need to look inside yourself and harness your inner strengths.

The strongest form of motivation is always inside you. You need therefore to discover yourself continually and find what you are passionate about. Once you know, follow your path and purpose relentlessly, and inspire yourself to do more and be more.

Conclusion

Once you have gotten your jealous tendencies under control, continue to strive to better yourself and your emotions. If you regress from time to time, rely on your family and your circle of friends for support. Share your feelings with your partner or your closest friends.

Write down your feelings in a journal and continue to motivate yourself to think and act positively. Write down all your goals as well and what you want to do for others. Make a chart of what you intend to accomplish and of how you intend to pursue your vision. Bring purpose to whatever you do.

Keeping yourself focused on the higher goals distracts you from the minor and insignificant irritants in life like being jealous. Visualize your goals and imagine how you will achieve these goals. Instead of being bogged down by negative emotions like jealousy, take the effort and time to create positive visualizations and affirmations.

Do away with the negative ones that rob you of energy and vitality. These negative thoughts and emotions just hold you back whereas the positive ones move you forward. You will discover that you have much more time at your disposal when you stop all the activities that had to do with confirming your feelings of jealousy.

Brighten your life and someone's day with a positive greeting instead of wallowing in self-pity, jealousy and negativity. There is power in words and that is why you need to use your words in a positive way and not in a hurtful manner.

Use words that lift up your attitude and the attitude of those around, especially your partner. You can have a positive and lasting impact on another person's life with just a few encouraging words.

Wake up to a brand new day every day and be thankful for that blessing and gift of a new day. It is your attitude that makes and breaks you. So, choose not to be weighed down by jealousy anymore. You do not even have to feel all great and fantastic every day. All you need to do is lift yourself and make yourself feel great today. If you do not feel it right now, tell those around you how you want to feel and it won't be long before you do.

Tap into that deep well of enthusiasm within you every day. Enthusiasm means sharing what you have inside with others. Enthusiasm makes you able to apply your powers and emotions and other gifts more effectively. It is that fire in your belly that tells you to keep going no matter what.

There are no such things as perfect relationships. In real life, there is no fairytale ending and no princess and prince charming. Fairy tales and romance stories are good material for books and movies but not for real life situations. Real relationships require work. Often, making your relationships work requires just that—a whole lot of work. But if you maintain the right blend of positivity and enthusiasm, then things might just work out for the best in the end.

Enthusiasm keeps you working long after you are ready to throw in the towel and quit. If you feel the little green-eyed monster clawing its way back up, kick it down and shut the door on it for good. Instead, lighten up and enjoy the moment while it lasts. Do something every day to maintain your newfound energy, your focus, your positivity and your freedom from jealousy.

Create precious moments with your partner. Those moments may be fleeting but they are what you will look back on when you are both old and gray. These precious moments are what you should be weaving instead of nagging at your partner about being unfaithful to you.

You do not need to plunk down a lot of cash to create memorable moments with your partner. A simple stroll down the park walking hand-in-hand can be one of those precious memories. Moments can turn your relationship from the ordinary and hum drum to the spectacular. So let go of jealousy and negativity and plan many precious moments with your partner instead.

Now, that you have come full circle, go on, and get moving. Free yourself from jealousy and live your life fully. Your relationship and your whole life is waiting for you to make the most out of it. Enjoy life free from doubts and negativity. Take it and view it for what it really is: a beautiful, precious, wonderful gift to be cherished!

Finally, I'd like to thank you for purchasing this book! If you enjoyed it or found it helpful, I'd greatly appreciate it if you'd take a moment to leave a review on Amazon. Thank you!

Printed in Great Britain
by Amazon